Tickle My Fancy

Creative Language Arts Activities

written by Julia Ring Alarie and Elizabeth Conlon
illustrated by Anita M. Smith

JULIA RING ALARIE received a Bachelor of Arts degree in History from Trinity College in Burlington, Vermont. She is an experienced language arts teacher in Essex Center, Vermont.

ELIZABETH CONLON received a Bachelor of Arts degree in French from Trinity College and a Master of Arts degree in Teaching English as a Second Language from St. Michael's College in Winooski, Vermont. She is a language arts teacher in Essex Center, Vermont.

ANITA M. SMITH attended Chapman College and Orange Coast College in southern California and the University of Colorado in Boulder. She is a graduate of the Art Center College of Design in Pasadena. As a free-lance artist in Newport Beach, she illustrates brochures, menus and newspaper advertisements and creates theme paintings for many restaurants. As a portrait artist, her specialty is children.

22971 Via Cruz
Laguna Niguel, CA 92677

THE MONKEY SISTERS

NOTES FOR THE TEACHER

The activities in TICKLE MY FANCY are for the primary purpose of developing creative thinking. Since children excel in different areas, we have included activities to allow children to express themselves in different ways. For those youngsters whose verbal abilities are more highly developed, the recording activities will be the most inviting, while the artistic children will be drawn to the activities using art or craft skills. For the writers and poets, we have included stimulating and humorous ideas to develop in varying formats. We encourage these activities to be an adventure in the unusual.

The presentation of the completed activity should be as important as the work that went into it. Sharing, speaking before a group and preparing a project for presentation are secondary skills in these activities which should not be overlooked.

While children may repeatedly select activities in areas they are most confident in, the teacher is urged to 'guide' the student to try activities in other areas (kingdoms) for variety. The PASSPORT is included as a method of record-keeping so that students will have an accurate list of the activities they have completed. It will also enable you as the teacher to see that the children select activities from each of the 'kingdoms' and try their skills in the different areas.

Each activity page may be individually reproduced or the pages may be laminated and made into a set of task cards for use as a center activity.

A reading list of fantasy books for children is included and this may be duplicated for students' reference. We have included titles that have been especially appealing to children we have taught, but there are many other popular titles that are equally as appealing. We hope this list of titles and authors will be the start of pleasurable fantasy reading for your students.

We hope this selection of creative activities will stir the imaginations of your students and TICKLE THEIR FANCY!

OTHER TITLES BY **THE MONKEY SISTERS**

SUNNY SENTENCES — Sight Word Activities to Cut and Paste (Grades 1-2)
SMILING SENTENCES — Sight Word Activities to Cut and Paste (Grades 2-3)
NOW CUT THAT OUT! — Math Activities to Cut and Paste (Grades K-2)
VALIANT VOYAGERS — Cartoon Booklets of New World Explorers (Grades 4-6)
SCIENCE ON STAGE — Four Plays: Ecology, Nutrition, Metrics, Matter and Energy (Grades 4-6)
SO WhAT — Spelling Only Without A Test (Grades 3-6)

ISBN 0-933606-05-2

the adventures

the kingdom of words — Writing

the kingdom of rhymes — poetry

the kingdom of sounds — Recording

the kingdom of color — art

the kingdom of crafts — handiwork

You and the Forbidden Mumlopi Fruit

On the tip-top of the Flumbop trees, the magical mumlopi fruit grows. It's been your job to pick the fruit for the Orchard Ogre, and you've been warned never to taste the fruit. Your curiosity has gotten the better of you, however, and today you slip one inside your pocket.

Write a story about what happens when you eat the mumlopi.

The Magic of Mossglen

Little did you realize when you stumbled upon this castle in the hills behind your home that you had invaded the mystical, magical world of Mossglen.

Write a story about the 784-year-old wizard who lives in the circular tower and the magic he has worked on you.

Tired of Tiring

"Hi! I'm Ralph Radial. I'm the one who invented the great new sport called **tiring**. It's fairly simple, actually. You just get six tires, glue them together in a column, and then you're ready to begin. Jump to the finish line without being knocked down by your opponents and you win!!"

Invent a new sport. Use some everyday item in a unique way. Write out a full set of directions for the game with a set of illustrations.

Stonehead

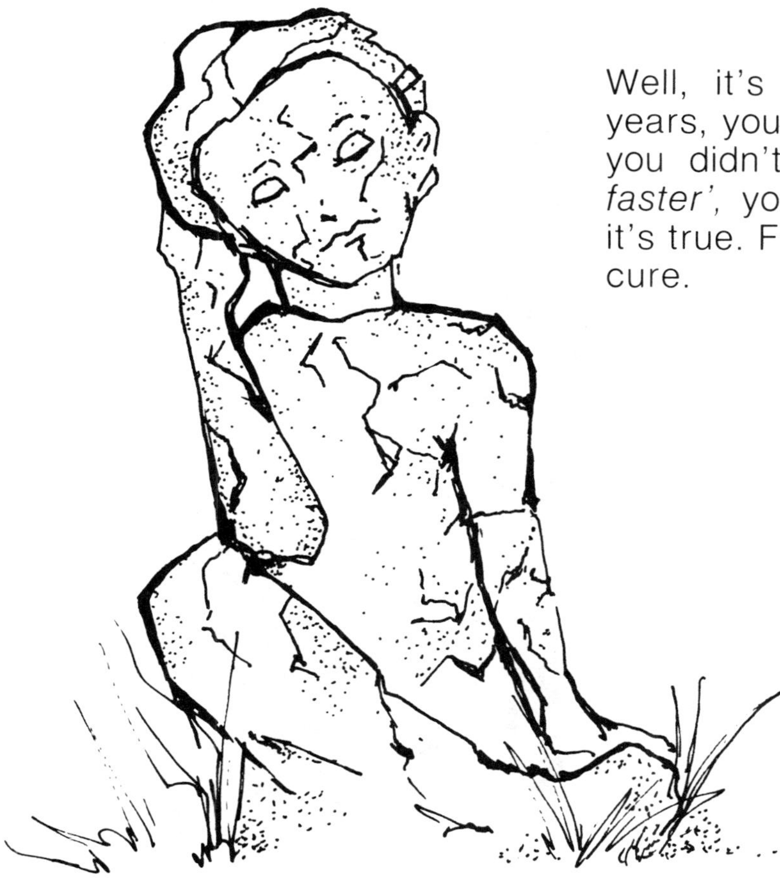

Well, it's finally happened! For years, you've been warned that if you didn't *'wake-up'* and *'move faster'*, you'd turn to stone. Now it's true. Fortunately, there is **one** cure.

Write a story about what you must do to return to normal. What have you learned from being a "Stonehead"?

Tootsie Training

When your parents said you could choose a pet for your birthday, they never dreamed you'd come home with "Tootsie."

Write a pet-care guide for others who'd like a pet like yours. Include information on feeding, training, and other problems which could arise.

The Castle on the Hill

Everyone in the city is too busy to notice the castle on the hilltop. But, you have seen it, and you know you *must* visit it. However, the way is steep and dangerous.

Write a story telling how you reached it, who lives there, and what they do for the people of the city.

The Royal Schedule

Remember that Lovely Lady who lived in the woods with seven little guys? Well, when she rode away with the handsome prince, they immediately got married and moved into The Royal Palace. It's been fifteen years since that wonderful day, and the Lovely Lady's life has changed a great deal.

Write a schedule of a typical day in the life of the Lovely Lady now. Tell everything that happens from the time she gets up until she goes to bed at night. What does she do? Whom does she meet? What does she eat?

You're Just My Type!

When the employment agency introduced you to your new secretary, you were doubtful to say the least. But he has done surprisingly well! As a matter of fact, you have just dictated a letter to the employment agency listing the advantages of having a secretary like him.

Send a copy of the letter to your teacher.

Forbidden Flimshun

No one has entered or left the castle of Flimshun for over 100 years. Everyone says that evil lurks within the walls. You, however, are determined to enter the gates and solve the mystery.

Write a story about the fantastic thing that has happened to the inhabitants of the castle of Flimshun.

Dwillie and Me

Earthquakes are caused when dwarfs leave their homes in the Inner Earth. Dwillie, the dwarf, meets a boy and they have a wild weekend.

Write one conversation the two might have had.

It's a Dog's Life!

Your two dogs have decided that they are going to get jobs and support *you*.

Write a story about what your life is like now that *you* are *their* pet.

It's a Deal!

After Jack chopped down the beanstalk and ran home with the golden goose, his mother decided they should move into a better place. They're living in this castle now. It's known to everyone, however, what stupid trades Jack is apt to make. So his mother watches him constantly.

Write a story about how you trick Jack into trading the castle for something you have.

Dinah Day

Dinah the Dinosaur is delighted! She has just completed a dozen daring deeds and earned the title "Dinosaur of the Decade."

Write a ballad about how you helped her earn this title.

Not "Eggs" actly!

When your mother sent you to buy extra-large eggs, you did exactly as you were told. Fortunately, they hatched just before you got home.

Write a rhyming poem that explains to your mother why you have no eggs and what you've got instead.

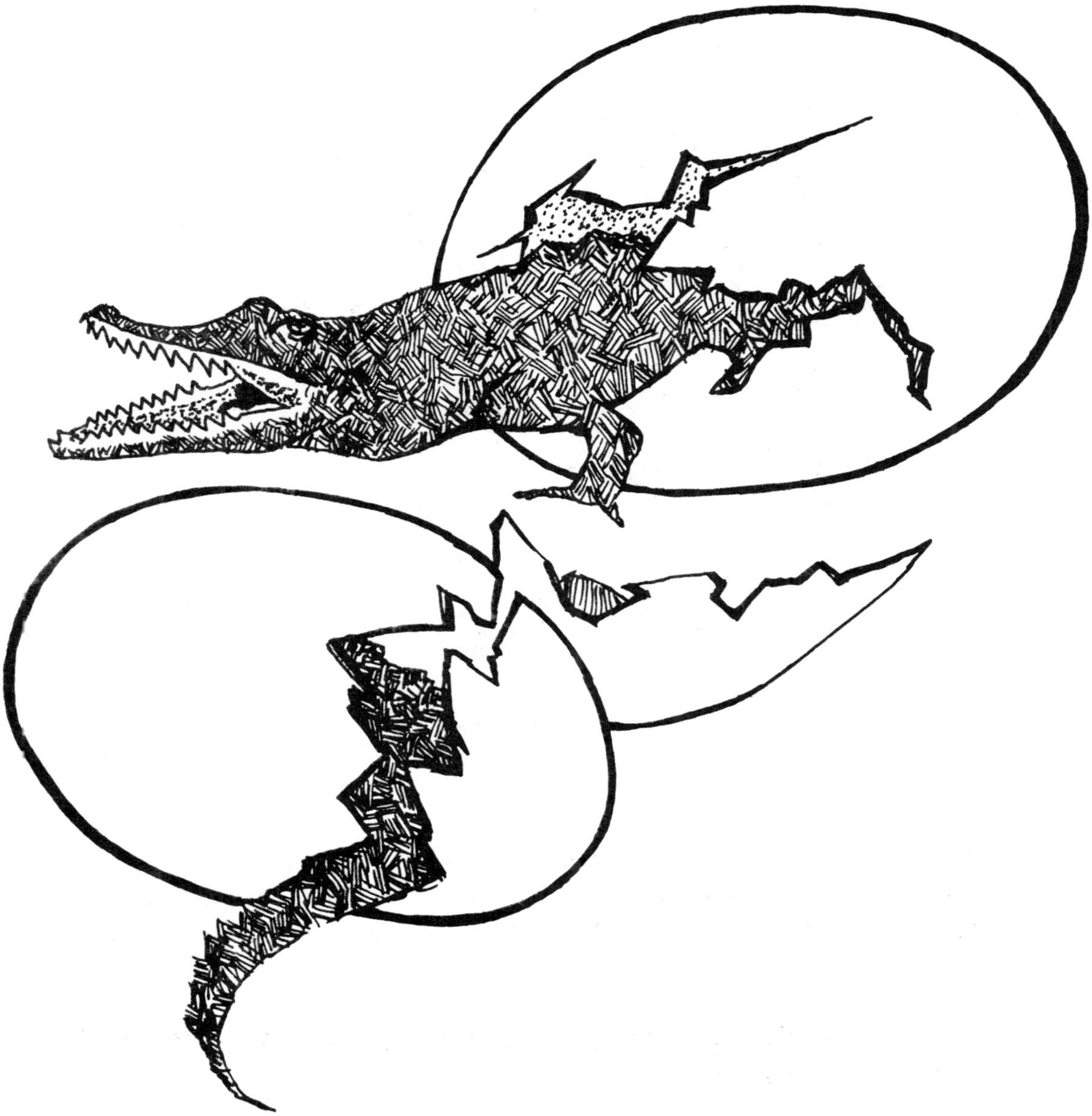

Long Lost Locket

You have fulfilled the dream of every archaeologist. You have found a truly valuable artifact: the long-lost six-petaled posie locket. But what does the writing engraved inside mean?

Translate the poem that tells about the magical powers of the locket.

Royal Remedy

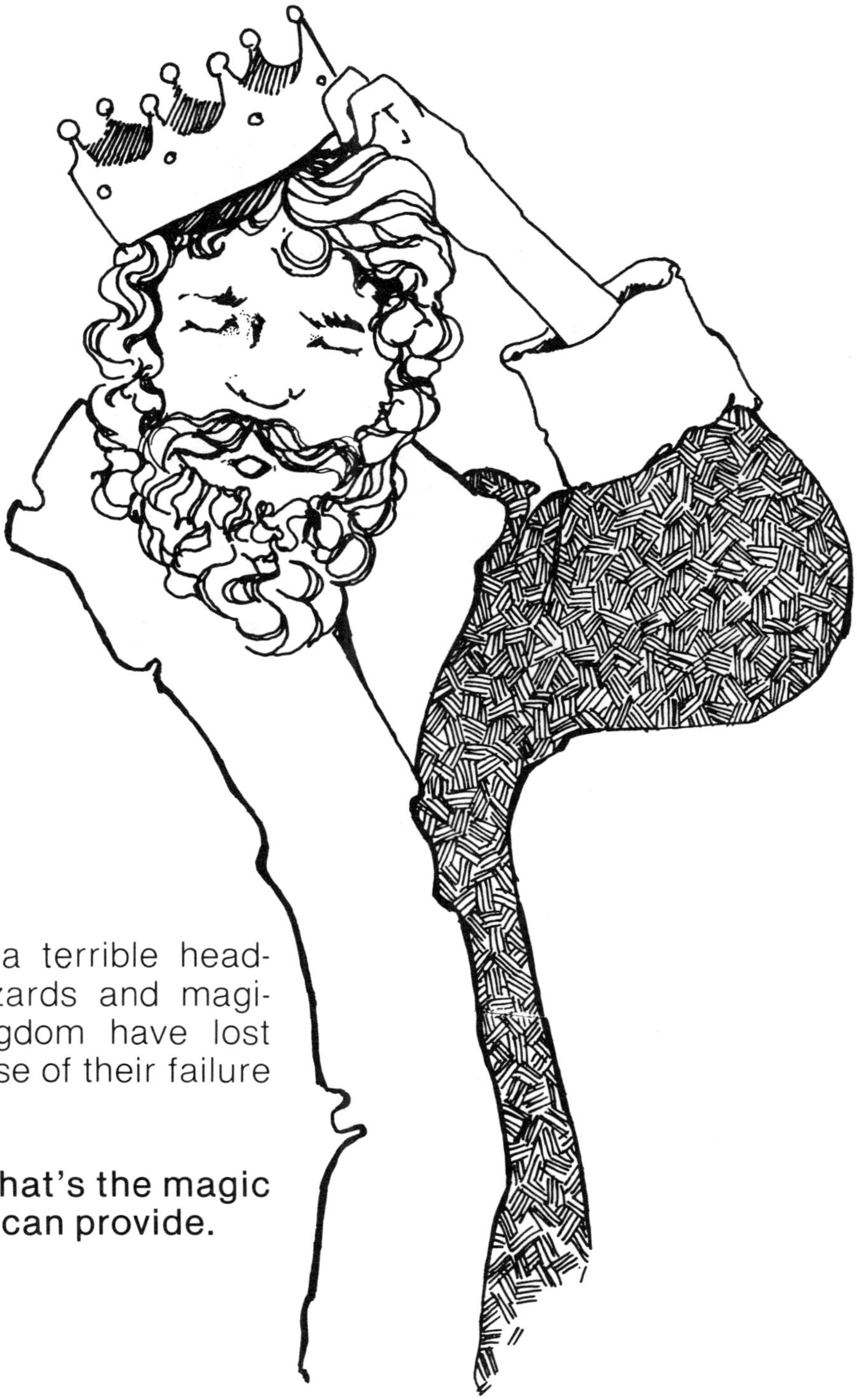

King Bosco has a terrible headache. All the wizards and magicians in the kingdom have lost their heads because of their failure to find a remedy.

Write the poem that's the magic remedy only you can provide.

Happy Birthday, Mother Goose!

Mother Goose is celebrating her 100th birthday.

Write a new nursery rhyme for her and include it in your beautiful birthday card you're making for her.

Pilaf Petals

Blow on the magic pod of Pilaf and its petals will scatter and then settle on different things in the open field. Whatever the petals settle on comes alive with feeling.

Write a poem about it.

Rockabye Hippo!

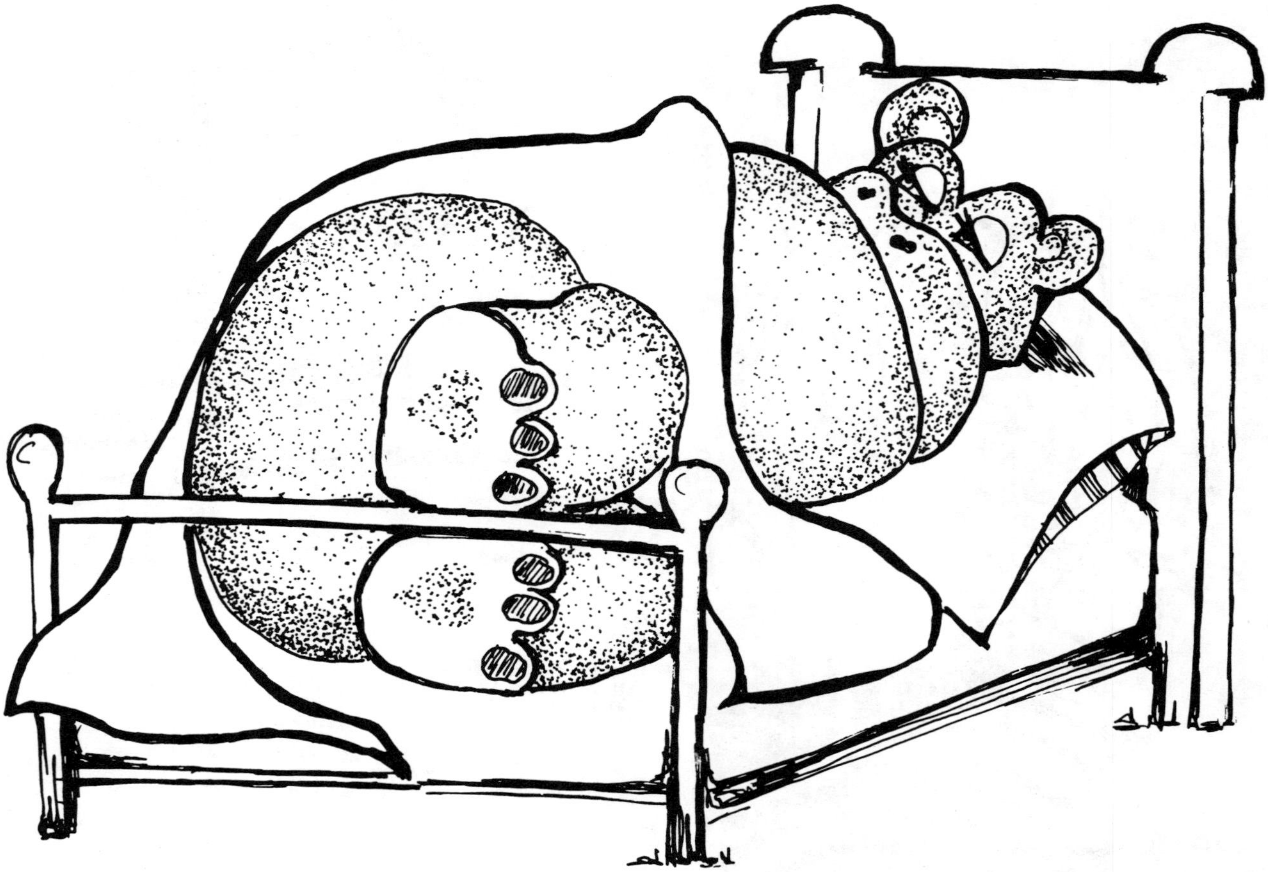

Your pet hippo can't fall asleep.

Record an original bedtime story to help him fall asleep.

Jumping Jennifer Johnson

Jennifer Johnson was the champion high jumper of Juno. She was last seen on October 23, 1978. On that dismal day, Jennifer was in exceptionally good shape. Her jumps were higher than ever before. Then it happened! On her final jump, Jennifer . . . .

You are an on-the-scene reporter. Record what happens as it happens. (Remember, this is a fantasy so use your wildest imagination.)

Toad Talk

You are sitting near a pond. "Well, what are you doing here?" You look around and see a small toad staring at you. "What's the matter? Don't you talk to toads?" To your surprise, the toad is talking to you and tells you his life story.

Record your conversation. What does he tell you about his life? How did he learn to talk? What will you do with him?

Hilarious Heredity

Grandpa has just received this framed photograph of his new grandson. Everyone has told him the baby looks just like him.

Record what Grandpa would say to himself about this whole situation.

Counting on You for a Good Story

Count Vampula loves listening to fantasy stories.

Write or find a story and record it for him.

Our Golden Anniversary

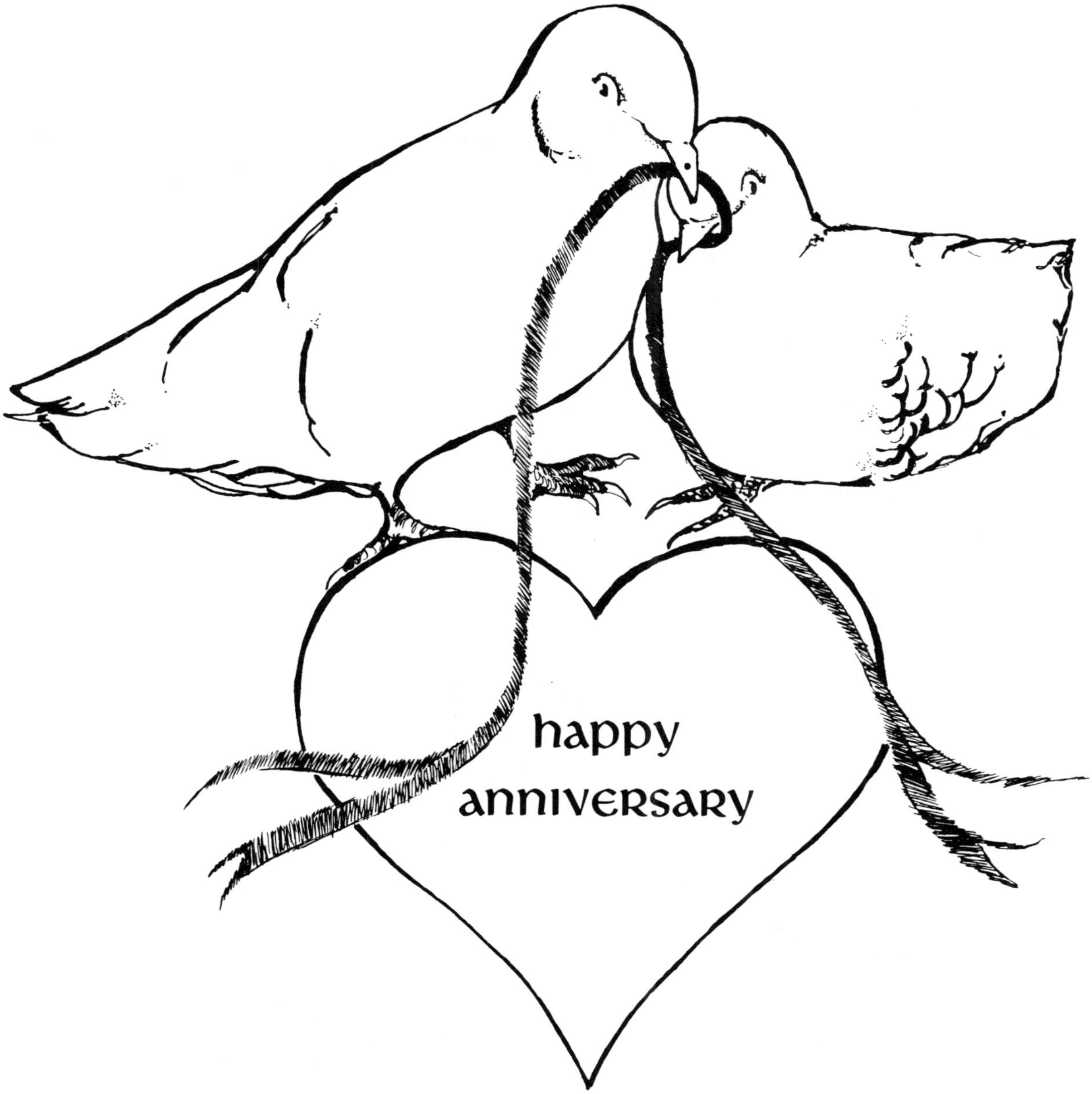

Cindee remembers that day when she left her mean stepsisters. Now she lives in a beautiful palace with Prince Charming. Today they are celebrating their 50th wedding anniversary. Each one is going to give a speech recalling his or her happiest memories from the past 50 years.

Choose one of them and record the speech.

Mapmaker, Mapmaker, Make Me a Map!

Up! Up! And away! It's a beautiful balloon! You are off to explore uncharted seas.

Draw a map as you travel over these unknown regions. Include any strange land forms and monsters that you see.

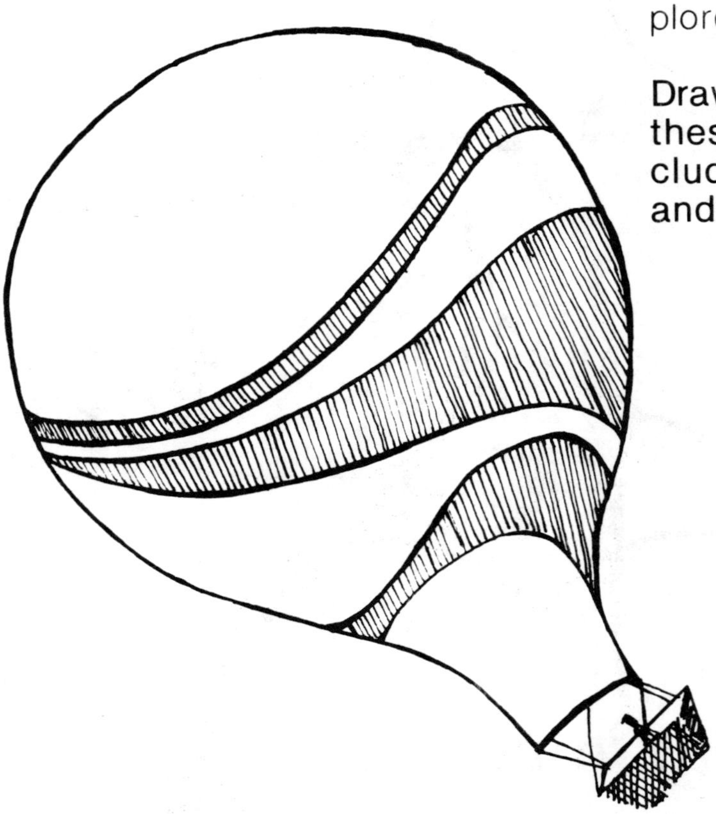

Cactus Woman

Out of the desert of barren dust comes

CACTUS WOMAN!!

She's the world's newest superhero.

Draw a cartoon strip of The Adventures of Cactus Woman!

Have I Got a Job for You!

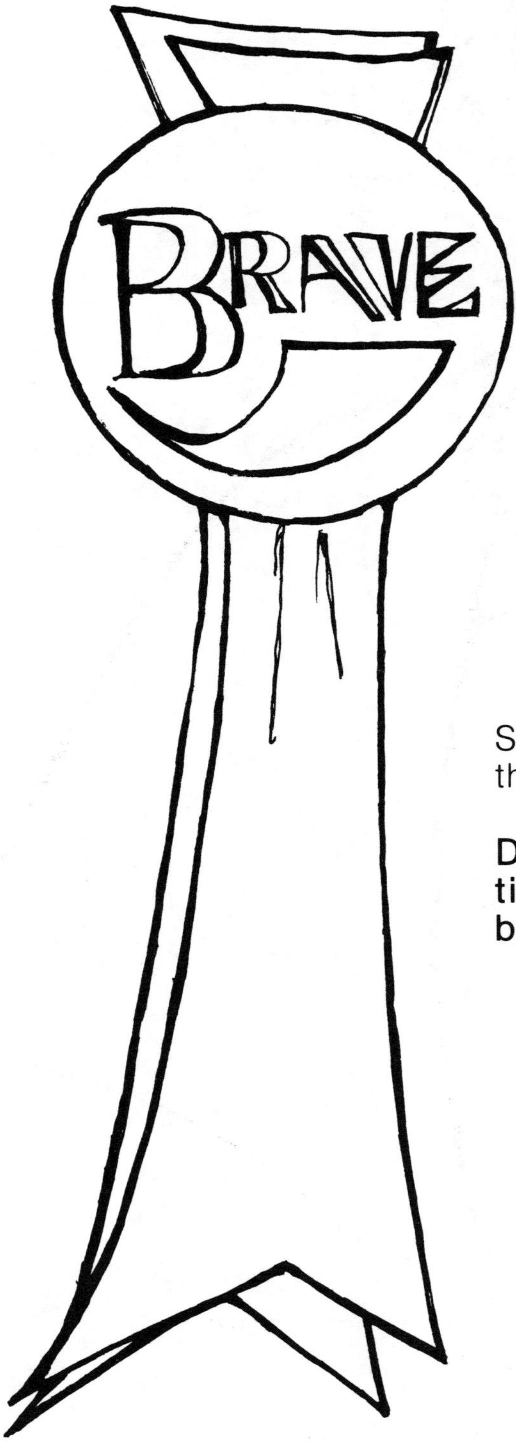

Some jobs take more courage than others!

Draw a cartoon about a situation that would really test *your* bravery.

The Pilary Palace

You've been invited to the Pilary Palace to partake of a fanciful banquet of exotic and unusual food. Everything on the menu is a new taste sensation.

Design and make a menu for this extraordinary occasion. Let your imagination roam to bizarre but delicious food. Use appropriate adjectives in your descriptions.

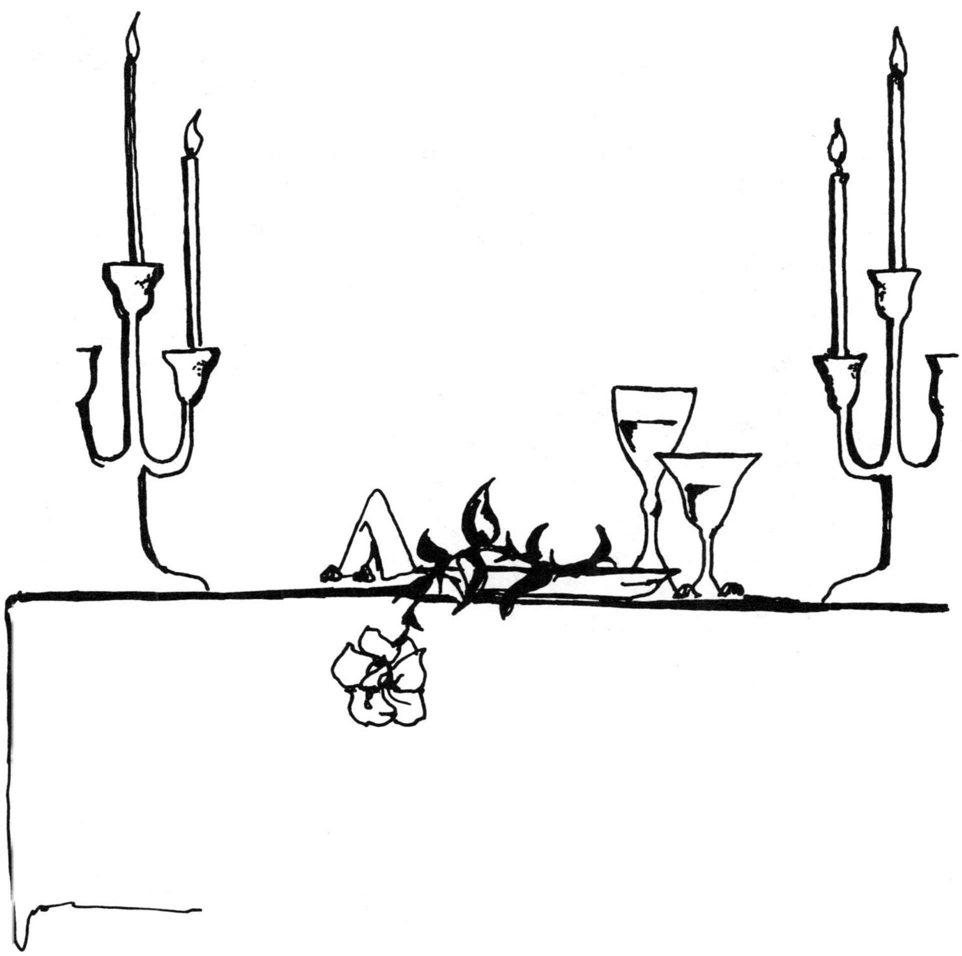

Just Chicken Feed?

Imagine everyone's surprise at the incredible growth of the baby chick your parents gave you. It's only been five months, but already the *'chick'* weighs almost as much as you do. Scientists the world over are anxious to learn how this happened. They ask you to fill a jar with the typical diet of your chick so they can analyze it as a potential food supplement for hungry nations.

Make a nutrition chart showing the contents of the jar.

Olympic Monkey Business

You've practiced longer and harder than anyone else. You've even changed to a special diet. And it has paid off. You are now the world's greatest gymnast!! However, there are some embarrassing side effects. You have a constant craving for bananas, your newly-grown tail tangles on the balance beam and you call your coach "Tarzan."

Draw a comic strip of yourself showing some ways that your everyday life has changed now that you are no longer human.

Be a Sport!

You are involved in sports every waking hour. Now it is beginning to show!

Draw a picture of yourself now that part of your body is some sort of sport equipment.

Algaenon

All night long, the waves have crashed against your ship, and the wind has whipped your sails. You are desperately clinging to the lines knowing that the end of your life is near. Suddenly, out of a raging whirlpool leaps Algaenon! What does he/she look like? What does he/she do?

Draw two or more pictures to show it.

The "Off" Spring

Spring has died. No one has experienced it for centuries. It is trapped inside this ancient witch doctor.

Make a colorful picture book showing how spring returns to us.

Fabulous Funland Amusement Park

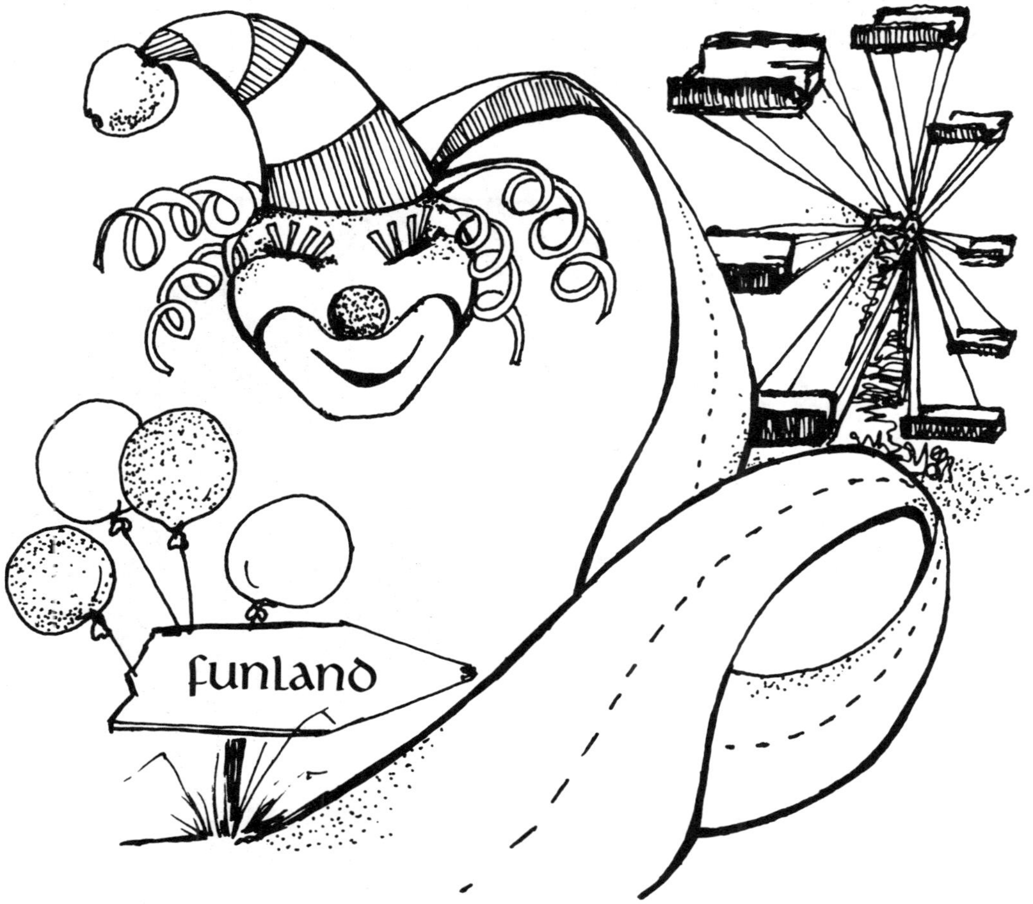

A very distant relative has left you The Fabulous Funland Amusement Park. As the new owner, you are able to design a fabulous new ride or attraction.

Make a detailed drawing of it.

Plot Your Way to Paradise

You own the *Whatatrip Travel Agency*. You specialize in unusual vacation tours. This season's most popular one is the 'Rainbow Route.'

Design a road map explaining how a person gets to the land over the rainbow. Include famous landmarks and roads to avoid. Include specific directions.

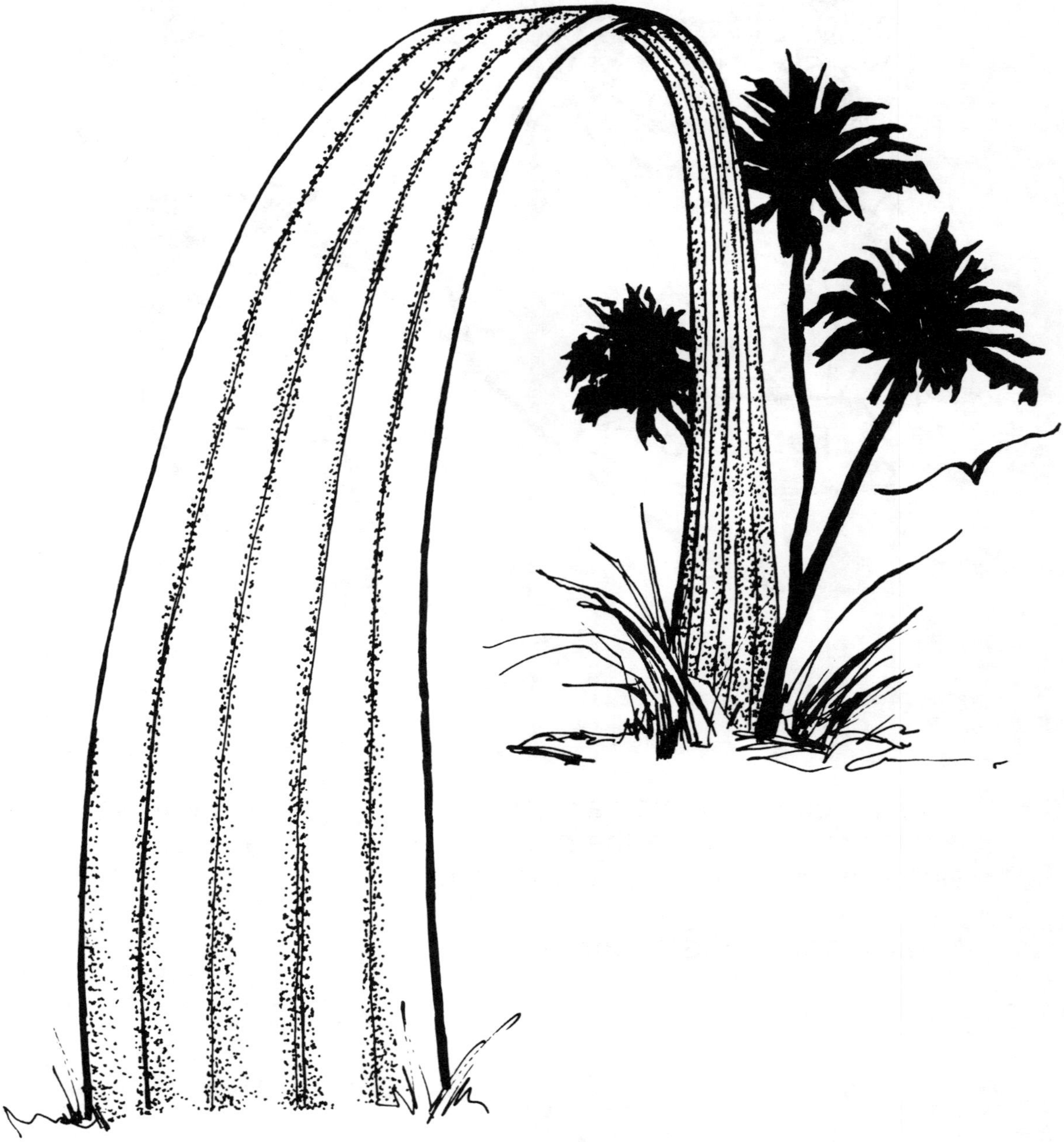

Midnight Fright

On the darkest, blackest
night,
When there is no moon in
sight,
Then a bluish, purple
light,
Shows a hairy, scary
fright!

Use black paper and colored chalk to draw a picture of the scary, midnight fright.

Write ten scary words that describe it.

FBI — Funky Beasts, Inc.

For the past few weeks, there have been reports that a strange creature has been sighted in your area. However, no real evidence of its existence has been found. You are taking your favorite shortcut home when suddenly you spot a strange impression in the dirt.

Use playdough or clay to make a model of the foot-print of this strange creature. Write a description of the whole creature.

Chilly, Clammy, Cavern Creatures

In a chilly, clammy cavern
In a putrid, pulsing pool
Lives a creature
Cruel carnivorous
And his friend, the
Fiendish Fool.

Make sock puppets of these two monsters and present a conversation between them. You may work with a partner.

Dragonmagic

This dragon, fanciful and friendly, comes to bring you all good fortune and joy. He scares away the evil spirits that could harm you.

Use a gallon jug to make a dragon-head to keep evil out of this classroom.

Suit Yourself

You've always wondered what it would have been like to be a knight all dressed in shining armor, but you have no money to rent a real outfit to find out.

Find things around the house to design a suit of armor for yourself. Model your outfit for the class. Don't forget a weapon!

Be a Clown!

You are the world's best-loved clown! The face you have created for yourself shows your true personality.

Do one of these:

A. Use a photograph of yourself and paint your clown face on it.

B. Bring make-up to class and create your clown face while you explain how it fits your personality.

The Fantastic Flyer

Here is Boris Malfactor, your arch rival. For as long as you can remember, both of you have been trying to develop a people-powered flying machine. Now his is actually in the air! You must have yours off the ground by next month or lose the title of "Fantastic Flyer" to Boris forever.

Make a model of the people-powered flying machine that will put an end to Boris Malfactor's desire to ever try to beat you.

Passport of the Five Kingdoms

Royal Seal

Date Completed	Kingdom	Adventure	King's or Queen's Initials (your teacher!)

I certify that I have completed the adventure-activities above.

____

Your Signature

READING LIST

Alexander, Lloyd, *The Marvelous Misadventures of Sebastian,* © 1973. E.P. Dutton & Co., Inc., New York.

Bailey, Carolyn S., *Miss Hickory,* © 1968. The Viking Press, Inc., New York.

Barber, Antonia, *The Ghosts,* © 1975. Simon & Schuster, Inc., New York.

Barrie, James M., *Peter Pan,* © 1965. Charles Scribner's Sons, New York.

Boston, L. M., *Treasure of Green Knowe,* © 1958.
An Enemy at Green Knowe, © 1964.
The River at Green Knowe, © 1959.
The Children of Green Knowe, © 1955.
A Stranger at Green Knowe, © 1961.
Harcourt Brace Jovanovich, Inc., New York.

Cameron, Eleanor, *A Spell Is Cast,* © 1974. Simon & Schuster, Inc., New York.

Carroll, Lewis, *Alice In Wonderland,* © 1968.
Through the Looking Glass, © 1968.
The New American Library, Inc., New York.

Cleary, Beverly, *Runaway Ralph,* © 1970. Simon & Schuster, Inc., New York.

Dahl, Roald, *Charlie and the Chocolate Factory,* © 1977.
Charlie and the Great Glass Elevator, © 1972.
Random House, Inc., New York.

Davies, Andrew, *The Fantastic Feats of Doctor Boox,* © 1972. Bradbury Press, Inc., Scarsdale.

de Saint Exupery, Antoine, *The Little Prince,* © 1975. Harcourt Brace Jovanovich, Inc., New York.

Eager, Edward, *Half Magic,* © 1954.
Knight's Castle, © 1956.
Magic or Not, © 1959.
Harcourt Brace Jovanovich, Inc., New York.

Estes, Eleanor, *The Witch Family,* © 1960. Harcourt Brace Jovanovich, Inc., New York.

Frances, Marian, *Witch on a Motorcycle,* © 1972. Troll Associates, Mahwah.

Gage, Wilson, *Miss Osborne-The-Mop,* © 1969. Simon & Schuster, Inc., New York.

Jansson, Tove, *Tales from Moominvalley,* © 1977. Ernest Benn, London.

Lindgren, Astrid, *Pippi Goes On Board,* © 1970.
Pippi in the South Seas, © 1959.
Pippi Longstocking, © 1950.
The Viking Press, Inc., New York.

Norton, Mary, *The Borrowers,* © 1953.
The Borrowers Afloat, © 1973.
Harcourt Brace Jovanovich, Inc., New York.

Offit, Sidney, *Soupbone,* © 1968. Simon & Schuster, Inc., New York.

Smith, Janet P., *The Ghost in the Swing,* © 1974. Steck-Vaughn Co., Austin.

Titus, Eve., *Basil and the Pygmy Cats,* © 1971. Simon & Schuster, Inc., New York.

Travers, P. L., *Mary Poppins,* © 1962. Harcourt Brace Jovanovich, Inc., New York.

Uchida, Yoshiko, (retelling), *The Magic Listening Cap and Other Folk Tales From Japan,* © 1955. Harcourt Brace Jovanovich, Inc., New York.

Williams, Jay, and Abrashkin, Raymond, *Danny Dunn and the Smallifying Machine,* © 1973. Simon & Schuster, Inc., New York.

See your local school supply dealer for these products by THE MONKEY SISTERS